HOW THE JUDICIAL BRANCH WORKS

BY NAOMI J. KRUEGER

The Child's World®
childsworld.com

Published by The Child's World®
1980 Lookout Drive • Mankato, MN 56003-1705
800-599-READ • www.childsworld.com

ACKNOWLEDGMENTS
The Child's World®: Mary Swensen, Publishing Director
Red Line Editorial: Editorial direction and production
The Design Lab: Design

Photographs ©: Denis Larkin/iStockphoto, cover, 2; Steve Heap/
Shutterstock Images, 5; Deborah Cheramie/iStockphoto, 7;
Pablo Martinez Monsivais/AP Images, 10; Tim Pannell/Corbis,
11; Alina Solovyova-Vincent/iStockphoto, 12; iStockphoto, 15;
Susan Walsh/AP Images, 17; J. Scott Applewhite/AP Images, 19;
Corbis, 20

ISBN 9781503809055
LCCN 2015919560

Printed in the United States of America
Mankato, MN
June, 2016
PA02309

On the cover: Judges sometimes use gavels to
begin court sessions or bring the court to order.

TABLE OF CONTENTS

CHAPTER 1

What Is the Judicial Branch?...4

CHAPTER 2

People in the Courts...9

CHAPTER 3

The Court System...14

GLOSSARY...22
TO LEARN MORE...23
INDEX...24
ABOUT THE AUTHOR...24

WHAT IS THE JUDICIAL BRANCH?

The United States was founded on certain important values. One of these values is justice. Many people pledge allegiance to the flag. They declare that there is justice for all people. The judicial branch helps provide justice. It makes sure that people are treated fairly.

There are three branches of government. Each has a different role. The legislative branch makes laws. This branch includes Congress. The executive branch enforces, or carries out, laws. The president leads the executive branch. The judicial branch interprets laws. This branch is the court system. In courts, people decide what laws mean. They apply laws to specific situations.

The judicial branch includes the Supreme Court. It also includes other **federal** courts. These courts handle cases related to national laws. States have their own court systems. State courts judge cases about state laws.

**The Supreme Court is the highest court
in the United States.**

Some laws are very complicated. The courts help resolve
disagreements about them. They also make sure laws are
constitutional. The U.S. Constitution is the highest law in
the nation. It explains how the government works. It also
protects Americans' rights. Other laws cannot violate the
Constitution. Courts can **overturn** unconstitutional laws.

Part of the Constitution is called the Bill of Rights. This
part explains Americans' freedoms. The Bill of Rights
promises many legal rights. In most cases, Americans

JUDICIAL RIGHTS

The Constitution describes the U.S. court system.
Several amendments protect legal rights.

AMENDMENT	PURPOSE
Fifth Amendment	• Protects people from being tried twice for the same crime • Protects people from having to testify against themselves • Explains the role of a grand jury, which determines whether to charge people with crimes
Sixth Amendment	• Gives the right to a speedy and public trial • Gives people in criminal cases the right to a trial by jury • Protects people's right to know about the charges and evidence against them
Seventh Amendment	• Gives the right to a trial by jury in many civil cases

have the right to a trial by **jury**. They have the right to an **attorney**. Attorneys defend people during court cases. They help people understand the court system.

Jurors listen to evidence and arguments in court cases. Then they make a decision.

There are two main types of court cases. One type is a criminal case. In criminal cases, people are accused of breaking the law. Jurors decide whether the person on trial is guilty. If the person is guilty, the jury decides on a fair punishment. In some criminal cases, people choose to have the judge decide. Sometimes, people are sentenced to time in prison. Other times, they must pay a fine.

Another type is a civil case. Civil cases do not involve crimes. These cases involve disputes. Sometimes, they are disputes between two people. Other times, they are between businesses. People or businesses can sue for money or services owed to them. They can also sue for damages.

Imagine an oil spill near an ocean. The oil spill was an accident. But a company was responsible for the oil. Animals were harmed by the spill. Businesses were harmed, too. Tourists stopped staying in the area. The businesses lost money. Businesses and people affected by the spill could sue the oil company. Businesses could ask for money to make up for lost profits. People could ask for money to pay for medical bills. A court would consider the case. Was the company responsible for the spill? A judge or jury would decide. Suppose a jury found the company guilty. The jury would also decide what the company had to pay. This process would provide justice for people affected by the spill.

CHAPTER 2

PEOPLE IN THE COURTS

Different types of cases have different procedures. But there are some similarities. Cases begin with a trial. All trials include a judge. Many include a jury and lawyers. These people have important roles to play. They help keep the judicial system fair.

There are several key roles in every courtroom. A judge runs the court session. In most courts, there is just one judge. However, there are some exceptions. The Supreme Court has nine justices. Like judges, the justices make decisions. They also direct court sessions.

Some cases involve bench trials. In these cases, judges listen to arguments from the lawyers. Then the judges make the final decision. They deliver the **verdict**. Most criminal cases are jury trials. In these trials, the jury makes the final decision. Jurors deliver the verdict. Yet the judge still has a key role. The judge sets court rules. Often, he or she decides which types of evidence can be used.

In October 2010, the nine justices of the Supreme
Court posed for a group photograph.

A jury is a group of 12 citizens. They sit together during
court sessions. Jurors listen to the arguments on both sides.
They consider the evidence carefully. Then they discuss
their decision. In federal courts, all jurors must agree on
the verdict. If they do not agree, the government decides
whether to try the case again. A new trial with a new jury
can happen.

A person on trial is a **defendant**. Most defendants hire
lawyers to represent them. All people have the right to an
attorney. But lawyers' services can be expensive. If needed,
the court provides a lawyer.

A bailiff hands a note to a judge. Bailiffs help
maintain order in courtrooms.

The **prosecutor** is also a lawyer. Prosecutors are used in criminal cases. They argue that the defendant is guilty. They always represent the government. **Plaintiffs** bring civil cases. The defendant and the plaintiff usually have lawyers. They sit at tables facing the judge.

Several workers help court cases run smoothly. Bailiffs apply courtroom rules. They keep courts safe and secure.

Judges enforce court rules. In bench trials, they
also make the final decisions about the cases.

Clerks manage court records. Court reporters record what
people say.

Most cases involve witnesses. Some witnesses are victims of a crime. Others have important information. They can help explain what happened. Lawyers on both sides call witnesses. The lawyers ask the witnesses questions. Witnesses share what they know about the facts. They **testify** about the case. Witnesses must promise to tell the truth. Their answers are called sworn testimony. Lying on the witness stand is against the law.

In some cases, defendants testify. However, they are not required to testify. The Fifth Amendment protects people from having to testify against themselves.

There are many people involved in the justice system. All of them help make the judicial branch work. The court system protects Americans' rights.

JURY SERVICE

Jurors are everyday Americans. They must be 18 years old or older. Adult citizens can be called for jury service. They report to a local court. There, they may be chosen for a jury. Lawyers ask questions about possible jurors. They want to make sure the trial is fair. People connected to a case cannot serve on the jury.

CHAPTER 3

THE COURT SYSTEM

Court procedures are designed to reach fair decisions. But sometimes courts make mistakes. Lawyers might question a judge's reasoning. Officials might overlook important evidence. People involved in a case can **appeal** the decision. They can ask a higher court to review the case.

The U.S. court system has three main levels. Federal cases start out at a district court. There are 94 district courts. Sometimes, these are known as trial courts. Each state has at least one. In a district court, a trial happens. A judge or jury hears the case. They make a decision. The people involved in the case might accept the verdict. They can also choose to appeal the decision. In a criminal case, only the defendant can appeal. In a civil case, either side can appeal.

There are 13 federal courts of appeals. If a district case is appealed, it goes to one of these courts. Appeals courts do

**The North Carolina Supreme Court in Raleigh
is the highest court in the state.**

not hold trials. They review records from district courts. A panel of judges makes a decision. In most cases, three judges decide. These judges are chosen by the president. The Senate must approve of each judge.

Usually, an appeals court decision is final. But either side can appeal the case one more time. They can ask the U.S. Supreme Court to hear the case. The Supreme Court is the highest federal court. It can make the final decision about a case.

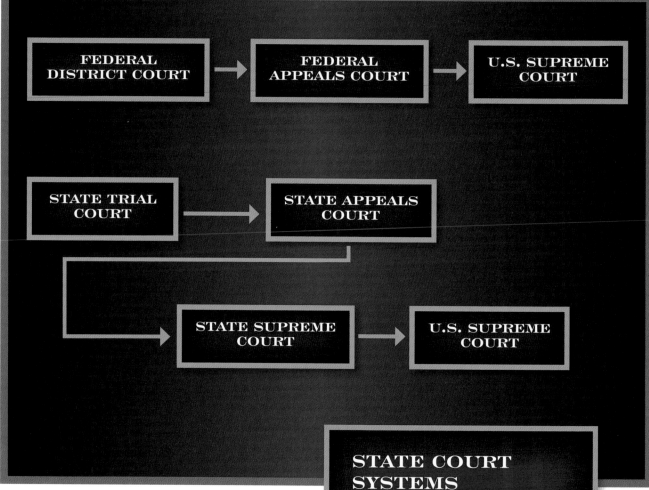

| FEDERAL DISTRICT COURT | → | FEDERAL APPEALS COURT | → | U.S. SUPREME COURT |

| STATE TRIAL COURT | → | STATE APPEALS COURT |

| STATE SUPREME COURT | → | U.S. SUPREME COURT |

STATE COURT SYSTEMS

Each state has its own court system. The lowest state court is a trial court. Many states also have state appeals courts. Then there is the highest state court. Many states call their highest court a supreme court. The U.S. Supreme Court is still the highest court in the country. Some state court decisions are appealed to the U.S. Supreme Court.

Many people try to appeal cases to the Supreme Court. Each year, it receives thousands of requests. The Court takes only a small number of cases. Most years, it takes

In 2009, senators gathered to vote on
a Supreme Court nominee.

about 150 cases. At least four justices must vote to take
a case.

Justices decide the outcome of Supreme Court cases.
Congress decides the number of justices. Since 1869,
there have been nine positions for justices on the Supreme
Court. There is one chief justice. This justice leads the
court sessions. The others are called associate justices. Each
justice has an equal vote.

The justices are part of the government. However,
they are different from other officials. Like appeals court

judges, the justices are not elected. Instead, the president **nominates** them. The Senate votes to approve or reject nominees. Usually, justices serve for a long time. They have life terms. Most justices serve until they retire. But justices must follow the laws. If they do not, Congress can vote to remove them.

Why don't people elect justices? One reason is to keep courts fair. Elected officials need to serve their communities. They try to make people happy. Officials might support laws that are popular. The justices do not need to make popular decisions. Instead, they can focus on the facts of the case.

Justices wear long black robes in court. They rarely speak to reporters. They do not often appear on television. But their jobs are very important. The justices take their work seriously.

NO CAMERAS ALLOWED

People cannot videotape Supreme Court sessions. They cannot take pictures. Many other courts also restrict camera use. Artists sometimes sketch the people in the courtroom. Reporters write what the people say. Some judges think cameras would harm the process. They say that people might see video clips of only part of a case. The clips could make them misunderstand the case.

In 2010, Elena Kagan (left) was sworn in as a Supreme Court justice. Chief Justice John Roberts (right) led the ceremony.

Before a case begins, lawyers for each side send documents. These documents explain the lawyers' arguments. The justices read them carefully. They consider the issues in the case. Then there is a public hearing. The lawyers give speeches. They summarize their arguments. Justices respond and ask questions.

After the hearing, justices discuss the case. Often, justices talk with their clerks. They consider similar cases from the past. Eventually, they vote on a decision. One justice writes

On the *Brown v. Board* case, lawyer Thurgood Marshall
argued before the Supreme Court. Marshall
later became a Supreme Court justice.

an opinion. This document explains the court's decision.
Justices who disagree can also prepare a document. They
explain their reasons in a dissent.

One famous case is *Brown v. Board of Education of Topeka*. It is also known as *Brown v. Board*. The Supreme Court took this case in 1954. In the 1950s, many schools were **segregated**. Black children and white children went to different schools. The schools for white children often had more money. Their teachers had more resources. Thirteen black parents in Topeka, Kansas, sued. They wanted their children to have a good education. The parents had lost their appeals court case. They won at the Supreme Court. The justices ruled that segregated schools were unfair to students. Public schools had to accept both black and white students.

Some Supreme Court decisions change important laws. Others simply uphold laws or decisions. Lower courts must follow Supreme Court rulings. Judges and lawyers pay attention to Supreme Court decisions. The justices' opinions help them decide similar cases.

The judicial branch is complex. It relies on many people and courts. These different parts work together to protect Americans. The courts help punish those who violate laws. They also defend people's legal rights.

appeal (uh-PEEL) When people appeal a case, they ask a higher court to consider it. Lawyers can appeal a case to the Supreme Court.

attorney (uh-TUR-nee) An attorney is a person who acts for or represents someone else. In court, an attorney might represent a person accused of a crime.

constitutional (kon-sti-TOO-shun-ul) When something is constitutional, it agrees with the U.S. Constitution. The Supreme Court makes sure laws are constitutional.

defendant (dih-FEN-dant) A defendant is a person who is sued or accused of a crime. The defendant usually hires a lawyer.

federal (FED-er-ul) Federal means national. Federal courts address issues related to national law.

jury (JUR-ee) A jury is a group of people who hear evidence and make a decision in a legal court. Americans have the right to a trial by jury.

nominates (NOM-uh-nates) A person nominates someone by suggesting that person for a job or task. The president nominates justices to the Supreme Court.

overturn (oh-ver-TURN) To overturn a decision is to change or reverse it. The Supreme Court can overturn laws and court decisions.

plaintiffs (PLANE-tifs) Plaintiffs are people or groups who bring a civil lawsuit against another person or group. Plaintiffs might sue for damages or medical costs.

prosecutor (PROS-i-kyoo-tur) A prosecutor brings charges of a crime against someone. The prosecutor works for the government.

segregated (SEG-ri-gey-ted) When something is segregated, it is restricted to one group. Schools in the United States were once segregated by race.

testify (TES-tuh-fye) To testify is to give evidence. Based on the Fifth Amendment, people do not need to testify against themselves in court.

verdict (VUR-dikt) A verdict is the decision made by a jury or judge. Each member of the jury must agree on the verdict.

TO LEARN MORE

IN THE LIBRARY

Burgan, Michael. *The Branches of U.S. Government.*
New York: Children's Press, 2012.

DiPrimio, Pete. *The Judicial Branch.* Hockessin, DE: Mitchell Lane, 2012.

Taylor-Butler, Christine. *The Supreme Court.* New York: Children's Press, 2008.

ON THE WEB

Visit our Web site for links about
the judicial branch: **childsworld.com/links**

Note to Parents, Teachers, and Librarians: We routinely verify our Web links to make
sure they are safe and active sites. So encourage your readers to check them out!

INDEX

appeals, 14–16, 17, 21
attorney, 6, 10

bailiffs, 11
Bill of Rights, 5
Brown v. Board, 21

civil cases, 6–8, 11, 14
clerks, 12, 19
court reporters, 12
criminal cases, 6, 7, 9, 11, 14

defendants, 10, 11, 13, 14
dissent, 20

federal courts, 4, 10, 14, 15, 16
Fifth Amendment, 6, 13

judge, 4, 7, 8, 9, 11, 14, 18, 21
jury, 6, 7, 8, 9, 10, 13, 14
justices, 9, 10, 17–21

legislative branch, 4

plaintiffs, 11
president, 4, 15, 18
prosecutor, 11

Seventh Amendment, 6
Sixth Amendment, 6
state courts, 4, 14, 15, 16
Supreme Court, 4, 5, 9, 10, 15–21

verdict, 9, 10, 14

witnesses, 13

ABOUT THE AUTHOR

Naomi J. Krueger is a children's book editor and a freelance writer. Her writing has been published in books and magazines as well as on the Web. Krueger received her bachelor of arts degree in journalism and reconciliation studies from Bethel University in St. Paul, Minnesota.